MONEY HABITS FOR SUCCESS

*Build Better Money Habits
to Build a Better Future*

BILL BLOOM, RICP®

RHG | MEDIA PRODUCTIONS™

Money Habits for Success:
Build Better Money Habits to Build a Better Future

Copyright © 2020 by Bill Bloom, RICP®

RHG Media Productions
25495 Southwick Drive #103
Hayward, CA 94544.

ISBN 9781735737096 (paperback)

Visit us on line at www.YourPurposeDrivenPractice.com

Printed in the United States of America.

ACKNOWLEDGEMENTS

This book is dedicated to everyone who wants to make their lives better. To the people who are willing to take the time to learn and educate themselves so that they can reach their financial goals.

To my beautiful wife, Jude. Your unwavering support never goes unnoticed. You are my everything and you inspire me to be a better person every single day. Te amo con todo mi corazon!

To my parents, Bill and Diane. You taught me the right way to do things. You allowed me to be myself and to learn how to better people's lives. I love you both so much.

To my brother, Joey. It was so fun growing up with you and it's been such a fun journey watching you become successful. I'm proud of you, brother!

Lastly, to our son, James. Son, the saying is true. You can do whatever your heart desires in life. Your mother and I will help you with everything we have. Always. We want you to be happy, independent and a thinker. We will always be here for you. You are our world. Love you, son.

CONTENTS

Acknowledgements..3

Contents 5

Disclosures..7

Foreword 9

The Beginning 11

How Money Works...21

Phantom Money 35

Fun Money 43

Keeping Score..53

Keeping It Simple..71

Bye-Bye Debt..79

Progress, Not Perfection.....................................87

The Way to Gain Control of Your Money................95

Retire As You Desire 101

Read These Books, Too!.................................... 113

About the Author 117

DISCLOSURES

The topics discussed and the opinions given are those of the author and may not necessarily reflect those of Woodbury Financial Services, Inc.

FOREWORD

By Justin Breen

Our brains are quite amazing. When we use our powers in our mind, magical things can happen. As an author, I write about . . .

Your future self depends, well, on you! Your thoughts, desires and actions all will get you to your future destination. The question is, what is your destination? Consistency. Repetition. Creating habits. In my opinion, this is how you create success through your daily life.

You wake up, get into a routine, and this can give you the opportunity to flourish. Abraham Lincoln said, "The best way to predict your future is to create it." When you know the future experiences that you are trying to create, you can have a way to plan for it. If you're not actively creating these special moments, what is stopping you? In this book, Bill Bloom talks about being financially able to do the things that you want in life. Setting a plan. Sticking to your plan. Using your own thoughts to create a better picture for yourself. These are all things that can lead you to success. This book is powerful because it shows you simple steps that you can take to make a better path. A path that is less taken. A path that is your choice. When you choose to become who you want to be, it helps to be financially ready to take on your future. Knowing that you can make a positive difference in your own life. I can relate to Bill's message in this book because it is all about committing yourself to a bigger and better future. Clayton Christensen, the former famed Harvard Business School professor, had a powerful statement: "It is easier to hold your principles 100% of the time than it is to hold them 98% of the time."

Your principles about money need to be aligned with your visions. Your future visions. If you want to have money for your future, being 100% committed about your financial decisions today will help you

pave the way for your tomorrow. By implementing your intentions, writing down your daily spending and goals, you set a path that you can go down to create that amazing financial future that you desire.

The habits that you can create from reading this book are designed to be a tool for you to learn from and repeatedly benefit from. Use the advice in this book. Set up your environment and surroundings to give you success.

Always remember where you came from. Remember those difficult times that you have had financially in your past. Utilize the tools and ideas in the book so that you can live a better financial life.

Justin Breen
Founder/Owner BrEpic
Author of *Epic Business*

THE BEGINNING

"Money is a byproduct
on how you want to live your life."
– Bill Bloom

Do you remember being a child? Take a moment to think about how you learned about money when you were a little one. Most likely, your financial education came from your parents. It came from the associations of your parents and family. It definitely did not come from pre-school, first grade, junior high or high school. Schools do not teach you about money. **The people around you teach you about money. It is my firm belief this is why wealthy people stay wealthy. They teach their children how money works at an early age. They learn valuable money lessons at an early age.**

Imagine if you were taught to save first and spend last when you were 5-years-old. Throughout your youth, you are enforced with a strong financial mentality to save first and spend last. Do you think your life would be different? Do you think you would be in a financially better situation? I know I would.

As a child, I had no idea what money was about. I had no clue what it could do – or how powerful or destructive it could be for one's life. I was taught how to play sports, study to get good grades and try to have a fun life. I was not taught about money.

My parents are wonderful people. They are the type of people who will give you the shirt off their backs if you need it. When it was the summertime and the mailman came to the mailbox, I would remember my dad asking him if he wanted a water or a pop. Those little things are what I learned from my parents. **Respect everyone. Respect your friends, family, the person helping you or serving you. We are all humans. It doesn't cost you ANYTHING to be nice. This was a very valuable lesson that I learned from the beginning.**

However, I did not learn about money. My parents were not business owners. They worked so hard for different companies so that they could give my brother and me a great childhood.

Were we affected when the job markets were not great? Absolutely. Did this affect our lives sometimes? Absolutely.

My parents were not taught money, either. It goes back to the good ole' saying: "Go to school and get a job." Generations of Americans have been taught this. Just go get a job. Don't take risks. Be safe.

I learned from an early age that this could NOT be a safe route. A company can let you go. You can get fired. The economy could get bad and you could lose your job. This was true back in 2008 during the Great Recession. This stuck with me from an early age.

When my brother and I were kids, we loved baseball cards. That was my thing. I would work at the concession stands at the baseball fields to make money. **And guess what I did with that money?**

I spent it. I spent all of it. I did not know a think about a savings account, stocks, investments or how I could make this money grow. The people who we associated with did not spend time talking about money or how to get ahead with amazing money habits. These things were not taught to me.

There was one major and important message that I learned by buying those baseball and basketball cards ... value. Rarity. Exclusivity. When I would find a special or limited-edition Michael Jordan basketball card, it immediately went into a protective sleeve because I knew there was value to this card. Finding an autographed card ... immediately went into a protective sleeve. Buying cards taught me how items could have value. I sort of self-taught myself that items could have value. And searching for these items was fun for me. **This has translated into me running my Retirement Planning business. Finding value for clients. Even though I did not have a financial education, I learned the VALUE of items.**

As one of my mentors, Mike Miller always told me, "Price is only an issue in the absence of VALUE."

Even to this day, finding items that have value is so incredibly fun for me. It has been ingrained in me since I was a child. To have extra money in college, I used to go to the Nike outlet store, buy soccer shoes for $50 and then resell them on eBay for over $100 or $150. I've always looked for ways to add value to an item. This is why I have so much fun working with clients. My goal is to add value to their money.

Imagine if each child was taught how to grow money in the public education system. What if kids were educated to save their money instead of spending it? What if kids were educated to invent and invest for their future? Our world would be a better place, in my opinion. Innovation would increase, ideas would be ever flowing and we would be teaching a generation to have a better financial future for themselves.

Companies, however, probably wouldn't like this too much. Why you ask? They would have less employees to do their work. You see, companies love having employees. The value in people is the value of compounding. If you have one person doing sales for a company, you could have a decent chance of being successful. If that company had 100 sales-people to sell their products, don't you think their chances of making more money would increase? Sure, it would.

Your job could set up a retirement plan for you. Maybe some health insurance benefits. Overall, a lot of people in the United States do not have a retirement plan at their work. How can you make a better future for yourself if your company does not have a retirement plan and you were never taught financial education? Sounds pretty hard, right?

Well, this book is here to help navigate you towards a better financial future. I've had to educate myself as to how money works. I'm still learning. Learning from successful mentors, constantly reading books and looking for opportunities to make life better for my family and others.

Going back to my time in college, I took a finance class. The teacher of the class was a financial advisor. This caught my attention. Someone who taught money for a living. This was very intriguing to me. I saw that he was successful. Showed up to class in a Cadillac Escalade that had a price tag of at least $75,000 or $80,000. Now, I have no idea if he was leveraging through his ears to pay for this, but it did catch my attention. We will look more into leverage later on in the book. This class was so interesting to me. Personal Finance. I had to have been 21-years-old at the time. In the meantime, I'd already set up bad money habits. It is very hard to start better money habits cold turkey. It takes time and discipline. I wanted to learn better habits. I started to apply what I was learning in this class and into my life. And as a 21-year-old, I just wanted to graduate and go find a job. As I graduated college in 2008, we went through the worst financial downturn since the Great Depression in 1929.

I knew that I wanted to become a financial advisor. I set it in my mind to have my own company one day. I never wanted to be told that I had to stop working or get fired due to circumstances outside of my control. I wanted to learn how to prosper during bad financial times or a recession. **There are opportunities when we go through bad times. I just had to learn how to utilize knowledge or skills during these poor financial times to have a better future.**

Deep down inside I wanted that for others, too. **I wanted to help others learn from the good and bad times that we have in our economy.** A lot of what happens is out of our hands. But that does not mean that you cannot take actions to help yourself?

The journey of financial education started. I took time to read books, learn about the markets. I received my securities licenses and started learning how stocks and bonds worked. These are things that we are not taught until we are in college, or for some, never at all. That is why people have a hard time getting ahead. They don't realize what they are doing with their money. They make thoughtless decisions daily that really effect their financial well-being.

Getting into better spending habits takes time. It is similar to going to the gym. Your brain is like your muscles. At the gym, you start off not being able to lift heavy weights or run for 5 miles on the treadmill without stopping. **You have to start small.** You have to build up to the 5-mile mark. If you tell yourself that you're going to lose 50 pounds in 3 months, it's probably not going to happen. You are putting so much pressure on yourself in a short amount of time, that you're probably going to crash and stop. This is a recipe for failure. Strategically, if you want to lose 50 pounds of weight, start small. Start with an apple and get to the gym twice a week. **The main item here is to begin. You must start. You must do. You must try. Start slow and steady.** Then, go three days a week. Then four. Build up your time in the gym or running around the block. We as humans must do. We must act.

The same is true for your money. **Getting bigger muscles or bigger bank accounts start with being consistent and having a plan. Starting small and making it a habit to save is such a crucial skill to learn.** Start by skipping purchasing that morning coffee (bring it from home instead). Pack your lunch. Give yourself a budget each week of investing and saving. WRITE DOWN everything that you spend money on! **Start training your brain today. You must start and act, slowly, to get better.**

It is incredibly difficult to say you're going to save $100,000 in a savings account or investment account without having a plan in place. Most people don't have the cash or the ability to generate $100,000 at a time to put into their bank accounts or investments. When you think about saving $1,000,000, you may think it is impossible! But, with planning and consistency, you can make it happen.

If you do not have financial goals, then you're probably going to go through life not knowing where you will end up financially. **Set goals. Be proactive in moving towards these goals. Don't leave them to chance.** Especially as you look toward retirement.

Here are the average retirement savings by age:

- Americans in their 20s: $16,000

- Americans in their 30s: $45,000

- Americans in their 40s: $63,000

- Americans in their 50s: $117,000

- Americans in their 60s: $172,000

https://www.synchronybank.com/blog/median-retirement-savings-by-age/

Ask yourself where you stack up against the above averages. Who wants to be average anyways? This alone should motivate you to increase your financial education by reading books, changing and improving habits, along with setting goals. **Almost half of retirees in America fear running out of money.** Half. That is a massive number of people who have not planned for a better financial future. Why is that? It is mostly likely due to lack of financial education. Lack of a plan. Lack of discipline in saving and investing. **Don't let this happen to you. As you read on, you are going to see how money works, how to think about money and strategies to help you get back on track towards a better financial future!**

https://www.aarp.org/retirement/planning-for-retirement/info-2019/retirees-fear-losing-money.html

MONEY STORY AWARENESS TIPS

1. The people around you teach you about money.

2. Did you learn to save or to spend money?

3. Are your financial habits serving you?

4. What money habits do you want to create that serve and support your goals?

5. Build new habits one small step at a time. This allows you to build up your financial muscles.

6. Be empowered as you read this book, lean in to discover how money really works and how it can truly work for you.

HOW MONEY WORKS

---

*"Formal education will make you a living;
self-education will make you a fortune."*
–Jim Rohn

I believe money is a byproduct of how you want to live your life. Let's face it, money can be a blessing or a curse. Whether you consider yourself, wealthy, middle class or poor, it is all about your mindset. You choose how money will affect your life. It is a choice.

One thing that I learned from Jim Rohn was mindset. Jim Rohn, who I talk about in other chapters, has been such an interesting person to learn from. I believe that your **mindset dictates how you think about money.** He said that "any person can afford to buy a $15 or $20 book that can change your life forever. It all comes down to your choices. You can choose to buy seven Coca-Cola's or you can buy the book that can teach you the ways to have a better financial future."

His theory is correct. The way that we perceive things has a major impact in our lives. Our relationships, our choices and our lives are all about choices. This book is designed to teach you about making better money choices. Better choices can lead to a better future. A better future could lead to a happier you. A happier you could mean much greater possibilities. See where this is going?

I've been very fortunate to learn from my friends over the years. When my successful friends recommend a book to me, I buy it right away. Does that make me different from most people? Yes. I love reading and learning. Why is that? Well, I want to be financially free. Forever. I never want to be dependent on a paycheck from a company. When you have financial freedom, you have control over your time. **Your time is your most valuable asset. Number one. When you understand how money works, you can have a better grasp on creating your own financial freedom.**

Let's get into why so many people struggle to understand how money works. The truth is, most people are never taught how money works. They are not taught to manage it, to work with it or ways to build a better and more successful financial future. They are taught to do well in high school, get into a good university, take out debt for a degree that you may or may not use and then go work for someone. Get a job.

During that whole period, from ages 14 to 22, you may have taken one class on business. And that's a maybe. When you were a child in grade school, there were no classes on money. You learned how to add and subtract, but you did not get taught how compounding interest works in your favor. Your math class did not teach you about how money could benefit you. How it could work for you. You learn the periodic tables in science class, but you did not learn compounding interest in math class.

I truly believe that if our education system would teach us business or how business works, we would have a much more abundant society. It would be hard for those who have never had a business to successfully teach it, but it could be done. **Learning about money could be the most useful part of your education.** Self-education is powerful.

This is why you're probably reading this book. To pursue a better financial future for yourself. For your family. For your loved ones. That is commendable. I wrote this book to give others an opportunity to aspire for a better future for themselves. It all starts with a choice.

Make the choice to pursue a better financial future. Believe it. Tell yourself every day that you can do it. Make it happen! Make the choice to be better!

Compound Interest[1]

I'd like to teach you about compounding interest. Here is an example of what compounding interest is:

Let's say that you invest $100 a month for 30 years in an investment account. Over the 30 years, your values will fluctuate because the price of that investment made will not remain the same every day. With that said, let's assume that you will have a

---

1. *This is a hypothetical example that is demonstrating a mathematical principle. It does not illustrate any investment products and does not show past or future performance of any specific investment. Investing involves risk, including loss of principle.*

rate of return or growth on your money of 7% after any expenses. Every year you will invest $1,200 a year into this account and if you are able to get a 7% return annually, what do you think your money will be worth after 30 years?

Now, this type of math is not taught to us in school. Can you do this math? Do you know how to configure this? Most people do not understand this simple math. You want to know why? You were never taught it! Again, the periodic table of elements gets used how often in your life? Most likely, never. On the other hand, you use money every day. Every single day of your life. It matters. Knowing how it affects you negatively and positively is the key.

So, what was your answer to our math problem? Here is a break down:

$100 per month x 12 = $1,200 a year

$1,200 a year x 30 years = $36,000

30 years x 12 months a year = 360 months

Annual rate of return 7%

Your grand total should be $122,487.65

In essence, your $36,000 could turn into over $100,000. That is powerful. This could be life changing. Knowing and understanding how this type of math can benefit you is a game-changer. There are really amazing free online calculators that can do this math for you.[2] The question is, how much

---

2. *Calculators are hypothetical examples used for illustrative purposes and do not represent the performance of any specific*

money do you want to obtain? It is simple to reverse engineer that with a financial calculator. Start practicing compound interest on a calculator or app. Start planning financial goals that you would like to achieve. Don't wait until you think you need to make $250,000 to start saving. Start now. Compound your dollars now. Your future self will thank you!

If you are a recent college graduate, you could have over $100,000 in your account if you invest ONLY $100 a month for 30 years and have a 7% return. This is not unrealistic. As humans, we don't pay attention to how we develop our spending habits. How many coffees do you buy a month? How many lunches do you buy a month? I'd like you to think about something: would you rather have money in the future or money now to buy things that you could prepare at home? This is the paradox in our society today. Many people can go out and afford to spend $5 dollars for coffee. I know I do it. I'm guilty of it too, ladies and gentlemen. Lunches, too. My wife and I like to go have a nice dinner every now and then as well. We are all guilty of this. Remember Jim Rohn's statement about the Coca-Cola and the purchase of the book that could change your future? The principle is the same here. **Where are you spending your money, every single day, that could be hurting your financial future? The odds are you are doing a lot**

investment or product. Rates of return will vary over time, particularly for long-term investments. Investments offering the potential for higher rates of return also involve a higher degree of risk loss. Actual results may vary. We strongly recommend that you seek the advice of a financial services professional before making any type of investment.

of unplanned spending that can hurt your pocket book, both now and for your future.

Now, let's take things a step further. Let's pretend that you wanted to have a million dollars saved for your retirement. A million dollars is your goal. You can reverse engineer how to pursue this goal with a financial calculator. Here is another example of how money could work for you:

In your Roth 401(k) you invest $10,000 a year. This means that you are investing AFTER-TAX dollars into your 401(k). You will pay taxes on these dollars that go into your 401(k) now, and you can receive them income TAX-FREE in retirement as long as you follow the Roth tax rules. Sounds pretty good, right?

Taking this example, a step further, in order to invest $10,000 a year, you could put $833.33 into your 401(k) a month. If you do this for 30 years or 360 months, you would have put $300,000 of your money into your retirement account at work. For this example, let's keep things consistent from before and use that same 7% rate of return on your money.

What will your sum of $300,000 grow to over your 30-year period?

$1,020,730.41

Millionaire. It is possible. Absolutely possible. Breaking down this opportunity is fun. You put in $300,000 of your hard-earned money and you could have $1,020,730.41 over the 30-year time frame. Who wouldn't want that type of return on their money? Especially having over a million dollars in your Roth 401(k), which would allow you to withdrawal money without paying taxes on it if you follow the tax guidelines. One Million Dollars Income Tax-free? Yes, please. Again, you're not taught this. You're taught to go get a job, go be safe, because that is what your parents did. This is such an archaic way of thinking. There are so many opportunities for you to go out and make a difference in the world and have your money rewarded for making the world a better place. Learn to set goals for yourself. By setting goals, you will start to program your brain to start taking actions toward said goal. The more time you spend putting these positive thoughts in your brain, the more effective your thoughts become. Your thoughts will turn into decisions and your decisions can lead to accomplishing your goals. It is up to you to make things happen.

As my mentor Jim Rohn says, "If you don't design your own life plan, chances are you'll fall into someone else's plan. And guess what they have planned for you? Not much."

Money does not always work in a positive manner. Debt can cripple a person's financial future. Credit cards make life very difficult for many Americans. The majority of people could qualify for a credit card. They can apply for one online, make a phone call or go to a bank to sign up, and voila, a credit card appears in the mail a couple days later. Most of the time with a promotion encouraging you to spend $3,000 in the first 90 days. Does this sound familiar to anyone?

Why do you think the credit card company does this? Psychology. Your mind will tell you that you need to spend AT LEAST $3,000. That is a lot of money. Especially in a short period of time. You are wiring your brain to spend. And spend a lot, on things you most likely don't need to survive. People think, "It's okay, I'm going to get bonus miles for my favorite airline! Now I can go on a trip! I'll need a new x, y and z. You name it." Brand new shoes, purse, clothes, hat or luggage. The list could go on and on. So now you are out $3,000, or more, of your hard-earned money to earn maybe $250-500 of round-trip airline miles. Do you see where the math doesn't add up for you? It adds up for the credit card company! You get into a mindset where you need to spend. And spend you shall. I've done it too! And I've realized it does not add up.

Now, let's say you spend $5,000 on that brand-new shiny credit card. You tell yourself that it is "ok" because you get points. Those points do not add up to the future value of your dollars. That same month that you spend all your money on items to get your airline miles with your new card, you get laid off. Now you don't have money coming in every month. The interest sets in for your credit card. It is very difficult to get out of paying credit card interest— roughly 25%. Your $5,000 purchase now becomes so much more than $5,000. Plus, you will not be able to sell those shoes, purse, etc. to someone for more than you paid for it. You are essentially buying a depreciating asset. You want your money to be buying appreciating assets.

If you pay only the minimum payment, plus 1% of the principle of this loan, it will take you 287 months to get this paid off – payments of only 154.17 a month. Guess how much interest you will be paying? It is astonishing—$9,735.87 in interest. Your $5,000 payment now costs you $14,735.87.

This is the problem with credit cards! Once you get stuck in the minimum payment/interest only payments, you have a really hard time getting out of that debt. Credit cards should be used ONLY for emergencies. NOT for points. Points make you overspend. Credit card companies and banks know this. This is a huge revenue stream for them. Please think twice before buying things on your credit cards, especially when you don't need it or can't afford it. It is not worth the stress, heartache and loss of future value of your money!

The reason why I am telling you all of this fun information is because people are living longer, and you don't want to outlive your money. **You absolutely want your money to last your lifetime or longer so that you can pass on assets to any heirs.** There are so many people who are alive on this planet who are over 100 years old. I know people who have reached the 100-year milestone. Actuarial tables for life insurance companies go out to 120 years old. That tells us that the probability of people living to 120 are growing every day with technology, medicine and medical advances in treating diseases. We need to retrain our brains to stop thinking about instant gratification and think about the next 30, 40 or 50 years of life – *or longer*!

Your coffee fix is costing you a ton of money as well. Here is the real cost of your coffee habit. If you buy a $4 coffee every day for 20 years it will cost you over $51,000! Imagine what you could do with an extra $51,000. That is the price of a Mercedes-Benz. And it is nice to be able to have a Mercedes-Benz. Especially when you can make your coffee at home for pennies on the dollar.

Now, let's talk about your mortgage. This is another clever idea that the banks came up with. Other countries in the world do not give out 30-year loans for a home. My wife is from Argentina, and they pay for homes there in US Dollars, not the Argentine Peso. Loans in Argentina for a home are really not used. Other countries have shorter borrowing periods for a mortgage and have higher down-payment requirements.

It is the American Dream to own your own home, but there is so much more that goes into buying a home. Knowing what your home is going to cost you over the time that you own the home is so important. Here in America, it is not uncommon for a person to take out a loan to purchase a home. Let's say a borrower will take 30 years to pay off their mortgage. That is a very long time to be owing someone money. And paying interest. Have you ever thought about how much interest you pay over 30 years? If you own a home in America, you should look at your loan origination documents. It will show you how much interest you pay over those 30 years. Please educate yourself and know what you're paying.

Now we will go through an exercise together on the true cost of a mortgage. The numbers will always tell the real story . . .

You and your significant other just found your dream home for $500,000 and purchased it. You couldn't be happier. You have this beautiful home. Your family can be comfortable in your own home. It is a beautiful thing. We all need a place to live. Prior to you buying this home, you and your wife decided to put a 20% down payment on your home. This means that you are paying 20% of the home value, which equates to $100,000. Saving $100,000 in cash is not easy to do in the first place, but you did it. When you do the math, your monthly payment will be $1,599. When you break down a $500,000 purchase to where it only costs you $1,599 a month, that sounds pretty good! You think that you can afford this. The $1,599 could not be an issue for you. But what about the interest? This loan is not a 0% loan. The banks need to make their money, too. If your loan has an interest rate of 4%, you will be paying a lot of fees over the 30-year period. When you do the math, again, you can use a calculator for this, you will pay a lot in fees. Your interest in this example is $178,737. That is how much EXTRA money you paid to buy this $500,000 house.

Your total purchase price for this home is actually $678,737! That about a 36% increase in costs. And by the way, this is not including your property tax bills, insurance bills, maintenance, cutting the grass and you name it. If you pay your home off early, you will obviously not pay that much interest, you will lower your total overall costs.

It is quite shocking to most people when they look at buying a home in this way. You could buy another home for $178,000! The same interest that you would pay to a bank, you could buy yourself another home!

Who do you think makes money over the 30-year period? In some cases, you may have to have a substantial rate of return on your home price to even come close to breaking even. Not to mention you need to have tens of thousands of dollars of upkeep for your home. A new roof, furnace, heater, HVAC system, appliances and many other expenses come up. Are you starting to see how debt works on the purchase of a home? Debt was made by the banks and lending companies to make them wealthy. Not you.

Imagine that you only put a 5% down payment on that same $500,000 dream home. You did not do a good job of saving every month for your future and you could only afford a 5% down payment. How would the numbers look then?

Let's take a look! You are buying the same $500,000 dream home. It has a pool, three car garage and a basement in an amazing school district. Again, it's your dream home.

You and your wife are now only putting down 5% of the purchase price, which equates to $25,000. That is still not an easy thing to do, to have a savings account over $25,000.

When you only put down $25,000, that means that you still owe your lender $475,000. That is a lot of money ladies and gentlemen. By only putting 5% down, you have now created an issue. Interest expense. A higher monthly payment. Less monthly cash flow. In this example, your new monthly payment for your home is $3,071! It is basically double. Isn't that something . . .

Now, if this were your home and the same scenario dollar wise, your interest paid over 30 years would be $353,751.

The total purchase for this home is actually $853,751. You would pay 70% more than the original purchase price due to interest. Again, this does not include property taxes, maintenance, upkeep and so on.

Let me ask you again, who is the winner here? It is nice to "own" this beautiful home, but who is benefiting from this? Are you starting to get how your money works? The systems put in place in our society are here to want you to go get job, which you probably don't like, making just enough money to get by. What are you doing to make things work to your advantage? Your money to your advantage?

Start by setting goals, by writing down ALL of your purchases and educating yourself about money. Your future self will be happy that you did!

HOW MONEY WORKS TIPS

1. What is your money mindset?

2. How are you choosing to spend/invest your time?

3. Invest time and energy in learning how money works.

4. Choose to pursue a better financial future by learning how money works.

5. Where are your dollars going?

6. Money can work in a positive or negative manner. How is it working for you?

7. Become aware of how money works, where your dollars are going and build a plan to support you toward your financial goals.

PHANTOM MONEY

---

*"Never spend your money
before you have earned it."*
–Thomas Jefferson

How often do you go to the bank or ATM and only live off your cash? I'd venture to say that a minimal amount of people do this. Most Americans live of their credit cards or debit card.

The problem with putting everything on your credit card is that you don't see the actual dollars being transferred from you to the clothing store or grocery store.

Your brain tells you that you will have a paycheck coming in two weeks. So, it is okay to buy this item now and you can pay for it in a month's time. The future value of your money is now depressed. It is less than what it could be. You automatically have a debt. You have now created a liability on your financial statement without knowing it. And you have reinforced the habit of having to have things now instead of waiting and saving for them.

Let me explain. When you buy a stock, you are buying an asset. A possible appreciable asset. This is a physical item that you now own. You are part owner in a company. Pretty neat, right? You can be an owner in multiple investments. These are physical assets that you could own.

When you spend money on a credit card, you are creating a debt. A liability. You owe your credit card company or bank money.

So, every time you swipe your credit card, you are becoming a debtor.

By definition, a debtor is a person who owes a creditor; someone who has the obligation of paying a debt.

You physically owe an institution money. Not fun. You are always in debt if you are spending on your credit card.

When you properly budget your money each month, you can let your cash make your purchases. This way you pay for things in the present time and don't have to owe future dollars to someone or some other organization.

My friend Hayden Humphry said it well. He told me, "The game is to become more aware, that is to say more conscious, of the things we do and who we're being while we do those things. When we become aware of something, we then have the opportunity to change it if it doesn't serve us. Otherwise, we continue in the same patterns, which operate unconsciously."

Let's say that you have $4,000 a month in income after taxes, 401(k), and health insurance costs. That is pretty good. Now, let's say you have $3,000 in expense every month. This includes your car payment, insurance, life insurance, mortgage, food, and your utilities. You now have $1,000 a month of free cash flow. That is a 25% potential savings rate.

That $4,000 that you receive every month is something you never see. It is what I like to call, "Phantom Money." The money gets sent to your bank. Not to you. Having cash like that is not the smartest thing to have laying around anyways. But, when this Phantom Money gets deposited into your account, your brain KNOWS that it will be there next month, too.

So, you say to yourself, I can afford this purse, jacket or pair of shoes. I'll have an extra $1,000 next month after my expenses. In reality, most people do not have the slightest idea on how to calculate how much free cash flow they have each month.

Want to know why? Credit card debt. They cannot control their credit card spending. Each month they are on a Ferris wheel of debt that never stops. Round and round they go into the world of debt.

The longer you have this habit, the worse it gets. It is extremely hard to stop spending money. It makes you "happy" when you spend money. It triggers neurons in your brain that light up the dopamine sensors. Dopamine is something that relates to happiness. This is why we constantly check our smart phones, emails, text messages and spend money. It all adds up to small and consistent triggers of "happiness."

But are you really happy on your phone all day? Are you really happy about that purchase that you made when you get your massive credit card bill every month? I bet the answer to those questions are a big NO.

Now, let's go back to your $1,000 a month surplus. Pretend that you have an automatic withdrawal taken out of your bank account each month to invest $250. And, another automatic withdrawal to put $250 of money into your savings account. Lastly, that leaves you with $500 of spending money per month.

Do you see how simple your life could be? You can automate your savings and investments and use what is left over to spend. There has to be a balance in your life. All work and no fun makes for an unhappy human! But, spending freely on things you don't need can really cause unhappiness and bad lifetime habits. You will have a very difficult time retiring if you don't have a plan in place to automate your future. Believe me, I've seen it and it is not pretty.

The reason why Phantom Money is so dangerous is because you never actually touch it. Digital banking technology has made our life more efficient. But I would argue that it has made people ever more oblivious to where their money goes every day. This is why you need to keep score and write it down. Every day. If you received your paychecks of $4,000 directly in cash and you had to pay for everything in cash, I bet you would not spend like you do now. You would KNOW where each of your pennies would go. You would have to physically keep track of your life.

Think for a moment or two. Pretend you have your monthly $4,000 of cash in your hands right now. How would that make you feel?

Pretty good, I bet. Most people don't ever hold that much cash in their hands. I also bet that you would be a lot more reluctant to let that money go!

This leads me to a question that I want to ask you: why do you let your money go, every month, on a phantom credit card? Why do you spend on a piece of plastic that does not help your financial future? The points that you accumulate do not add up to savings. They actually help you spend more.

Starting to use physical cash every month can help you get ahead and keep score in a more effective manner. A client of mine taught me this trick years ago. They both live on pensions and their social security. They do not need to spend all of their money from their retirement incomes each month. They save money. They have fun with this. They put $500 a month of cash in an envelope. That is their play money. If they want to go out to eat, they use those monies to do so. If they want to go have a drink, they use those monies. That envelope is their play money envelope. And when you have physical currency, not Phantom Money, you are so much more aware of your financial well-being. When the envelope is empty for the month, then you have to wait until the next monthly allotment for additional spending money for things like entertainment, dinners out, new shoes etc. This is how you can balance having fun in the now without going into debt and sabotaging your future.

That cash allows them to have consistent spending habits. It also allows them to save money! Yes, save money. Parting with physical money is a lot more painful than swiping your credit card freely. Using physical money helps you create a true connection and awareness of your money, earning it and spending it in ways that are more meaningful for you.

You, too, could put yourself in a better financial position by having a cash budget every month. You could set up a spending envelope that will allow you to have fun and enjoy your life. And if you want to buy a new suit or a pair of shoes, you could save money in that envelope to buy that item. Be precise with your money. Or, **you could buy investments with your money and let the money work for you. This is what the wealthy do with their money. They let it work for them and pay for their items this way.** The wealthy save and invest first and spend second. You, too, can do this.

Automate, budget and spend what is left. Save and invest first!

MONEY TIPS

1. Be aware of where your money is going.

2. Beware of phantom money. Just because you don't see or touch it doesn't mean the way you spend it doesn't matter. Your spending habits can hurt or help you meet your financial goals.

3. Put a boundary around your spending each month. (Not the credit card company limits.)

4. Create an envelope of spending cash for the month--and honor it. Once its empty, you stop spending for the month.

5. Budget and automate. In fact, save and invest first!

FUN MONEY

There is a plethora of positive attributes of money:

Financial Freedom.

Time, which is truly our most valuable asset, in my humble option.

Purpose.

Giving.

You name it.

In our world, there are many generous people. Look at Oprah. The Queen of giving. You can truly build an empire by doing what you love. She is a great example of this. Do you remember what she would give away during her TV shows? Some of the most amazing things that she gave away were diamond watches, seven-day cruises, even a VW Beetle! Think about that . . . she gave every member of her audience a new car.

That is powerful.

Wealth can be used for the good of mankind. Think about how Oprah must have felt when she gave these gifts to her audiences. Probably pretty amazing. She did this out of the kindness of her heart. Did it help her ratings, sure? Did it help her business? Possibly. She knew how to make it count. Giving is in her DNA.

Robert F. Smith, another billionaire, paid off the student loan debt of an entire graduating class at Morehouse College. How amazing. Just the pure fact that he decided to spend hundreds of thousands or millions of dollars to help these students was extremely generous.

Money can be used in positive ways in our lives. Accumulating large sums of money is the result of what you tell yourself between your two ears every day. How you think about money will affect how much you have. The legendary book, *Think and Grow Rich* by Napoleon Hill is a prime example of this. He spent 25-years of his life researching and documenting the practices of very wealthy business people in the early 20th century. If you have not read this book, I would highly recommend it. His life's dedication to this topic of money and successful entrepreneurs has led thousands of people down a better financial path.

When you become fortunate enough to have these large sums of money, giving becomes even more powerful. It becomes fun.

The thing is, you don't need a large sum of money to give and help others. Sending a warm meal to someone in need feels good. Giving feels good. That is why we do it as humans. The more money that you accumulate translates into more giving that you could accomplish.

Jim Rohn is a legend in my mind. I wish he was still alive. I would have loved to of met him. He is a mentor of mine through his audiobooks and seminars. I listen to his recordings weekly. Some more than others, but every week I listen to at least an hour of his speeches. He was a brilliant man and an even better communicator.

In one of his speeches, he said something so remarkable that it really got me thinking. He mentioned that he hears people all the time say that if they only had a million dollars or won the lottery, that they would STOP working. They would stop everything that they are currently doing. And my friends, this is why the good Lord does not grant them with this wish. They would stop working. Stop contributing.

I believe we are meant to give and contribute. Our ancestors worked day and night with a fraction of the comforts that we now possess in today's world. All with less money than we have now. We were meant to be there for others, to give and to be kind.

Once you reach certain monetary levels, it still costs you absolutely nothing to be nice to others. I really think that gets overlooked in today's fast-paced environment.

As you do become wealthier by keeping track of your money, you now have new opportunities to have fun. Opportunities could find you, too. You could use your wealth to help others. Create new companies. Create jobs. You could help put food on other's plates. The possibilities are endless.

That is powerful.

Creation. Creativity.

You see, money does not have to be evil. It does not always mean greed. There are truly amazing people out there that would give you the shirt off their backs and they don't have much money at all.

My view about money is quite simple. **Write things down—simple. Keep track—simple**. Align your spending with your goals both short-term and long-term. Do you see a trend? I'm a simplifier by nature. It is just how my brain works. If you want riches, you must first understand where your money is going. I truly believe this.

As Dr. Kevin Elko says, "Be where your feet are." How powerful is that? Be present and aware as to where your money is going.

Now, look at the role that money plays in your own life. Have you had to not go on vacation for the past couple of years because you didn't have the funds? I'm sure a lot of people would say yes.

Or, did you go on that vacation, overspend, because you did not allocate funds for this? I bet this has a higher probability of a yes answer.

The facts are obvious. You need to be honest with yourself. Honest with your spending. Your saving, or lack thereof. Then choose how you want your future spending to look going forward and spend, invest and save in alignment with your goals.

We, as humans, are what we tell ourselves. The view that we have of ourselves is really, really important. In Hill's book, he writes about the steel magnate, Andrew Carnegie. Carnegie wrote about how he dreamed of his fortunes. His dreams became a reality because he literally thought and grew rich. He used his visions to amass a sizeable fortune. He ended up donating his fortune in the later parts of his life.

How do you feel about money? Positively? Negatively?

A lot of these thoughts probably came from your parents and your surroundings growing up. How you think about money drastically impacts your financial future.

If you think money is the root of all evil, you're right.

If you think money is a tool that can help you have a better life, you're right. What are you choosing to believe?

You see, it is all about what you tell yourself. The closest people around you have an impact on your financial education and thoughts as well. This could be positive or dangerous and you don't even know it.

Our closest friends have a big impact on our finances. We just don't realize it. We have all had a person in our lives at one point or another that did not help your financial future. They would ask you to get drinks multiple times a week after work. **Or go to Starbucks twice a day AND go out to lunch**

daily. Forty years of this could make or break your ability to be able to Retire As You Desire.

Bad habits are the enemy. Writing down what you spend can be your best friend for your future.

Be kind to yourself. Be kind to your future financial self. Take the time today to get in a better financial situation.

Write down how much money you would like to have by when. You absolutely should put a deadline on this goal. You brain will begin to think of ways to make this happen. **Set goals with timeframes.**

Please do not go through life without setting goals for yourself. Especially financial goals. If you are still a student and are reading this book, congratulations. You are taking a proactive step towards your goal of an amazing financial future for yourself. This is the best time to create amazing money habits.

By knowing what you want and setting goals, you can put steps in place to make them happen. Remember, you don't have to do this alone. Get help from your Financial Advisor to set goals and build a plan.

Think of your goal. Write it down. Read books like this and the ones that I have mentioned throughout this book. Surround yourself with financially stable and literate people. Keep track of your money, daily. Ask a successful person to go have lunch with you. Ask them about their story. People love sharing their story and being heard. **Most successful people are happy to share their secrets to success. It**

probably won't be a big secret at all. They set goals. They work toward them. They keep track of them daily and make things happen. You can do this, too!

(At the end of this book, I have a list of other books that have influenced my financial life that I would highly recommend you to read.)

When you set goals and achieve them, it gives you an opportunity to celebrate your wins. Celebrate life. Life is worth celebrating.

When you truly have a system in place to help you with your financial life, it could free up time for you to do even more things:

Explore.

Travel.

Be financially free.

Think about this . . . when you get your financial house in order, you can plan for fun. You can actually go out and afford to have fun. You could be able to budget and save for that trip that you always wanted to go on.

If that isn't exciting and motivating, I don't know what is! Build your plan and build your financial freedom, fun money and great giving into your life.

You, yes, you, can make money fun.

It is a choice. You can make it a game. Make it exciting. Make it fun. Enjoy the ride!

When I work with my soon-to-be retired clients, planning their retirement income is what I love to do the most.

When I am able to plan for someone to have $5,000, $8,000 or $10,000 of income that can last the rest of their lives, that's FUN!

You don't need to wait until retirement to have your money work for you in this manner. Start today. Be consistent. Build your plan and make it meaningful and fun!

FUN MONEY TIPS

1. Wealth can be used for good.

2. Track your spending and build positive money habits.

3. Align your spending with your goals.

4. Pay attention to what you are telling yourself and believe about money.

5. Surround yourself with those who can empower you and your relationship with money.

6. Tap into the wisdom and insights available to you from successful experts.

7. Build, plan and have fun!

KEEPING SCORE

"The path to success is to take massive,
determined action."
–Tony Robbins

Today I spent $454.76. This could be an average day for me. I'm a business owner and I definitely have expenses. Today I sent out some gift baskets for clients, diapers to a friend who recently had a baby and something for my wonderful wife. In my daily journal, I write down every penny that I spend money on. I keep score.

This exercise of writing down everything that I spend money on is not easy. There are still days that I forget to do this. But this has made me so much more aware of my spending.

We live in such a face paced environment, that we tend to forget what we spend money on. When is the last time that you focused your attention on your spending? Where are your dollars actually going?

If you are like most people, the answer to that is probably never.

When you don't keep score, you never get ahead.

> *"When performance is measured, performance improves. When performance is measured and reported back, the rate of improvement accelerates."*
> — *Pearson's Law*

It is my belief that without a plan, you cannot get ahead. And without a measurement tool keeping score, you won't have a clue where your financial future lies. Getting lucky by inheriting money or winning the lottery will not solve your money issues. Soon, those monies could disappear due to your lack of financial education.

I believe YOU are your money issue. Yes, you! When you look in the mirror, you need to realize that you are responsible for your spending. No one else. You are in control of your funds. Therefore, you are also your money solution!

This is true if you are in high school and working a part-time job or a 40-year-old professional who has been working for 18 years.

Most people unconsciously spend and let their hard-earned dollars disappear. Credit cards are the worst when it comes to unconsciously spending. Believe me, I know. I've been there, too. I'm still working on this habit. Credit cards are the enemy of keeping score. Having a bill due in 30 days really hurts your future cash flow. It suffocates your future investing potential, too. If you have a $5,000 a month credit card bill, how much of that is actually needed? Most likely, a small amount of it. Try using cash, let's say, $500 a month and spend off of that. Put your credit card away for real emergencies. That was originally the purpose of credit cards.

If you could save $4,500 a month in being more aware of your spending habits and invest that money, pretty soon your investments could be paying for your vacations and cars. Your assets, your money, could be working for you, instead of you working for it. The wealthy build companies or opportunities to have money work for them, have people work for them. They keep score by their profits.

And profits are greater than an income. Keep score of your profits.

A handful of times in my career, I've seen people blow through an inheritance. When a client of mine would unfortunately pass and their beneficiaries would inherit money, there were only two outcomes. In my experiences, the beneficiaries with little to no financial education usually spent all the money that they just inherited within one to three years. They were not keeping score. They did not see the long-term potential of their new-found wealth. It is sad. They think only of today.

One time, a client's son blew $250,000 within the first couple months of inheriting the money. Remember, if you are not keeping score, you could have a big tax bill to pay, which I warned him of, but to no avail. He withdrew all of the funds and went on a spending spree. Pretty soon he was scrambling for money to pay his tax bill the following year. It was not a pretty sight.

Having a new truck or BMW in your driveway does not make you wealthy. It usually is such a liability that you do not understand the negative consequences. Again, lack of score keeping. Again, lack of discipline.

The others that tracked their dollars (knew how to keep score), made plans of how to invest and plan for the future with the inheritance, were able to shift their financial picture powerfully both in the present and the future. Build the practice of keeping score.

When I was 22, and done with college, I had about $54,000 in student loan debt. I started my career in 2008. The least optimal time to graduate college and get a job. We were in a terrible recession here in America due to a banking financial crisis. When I started working at Prudential as a Financial Advisor, I had no income. Not one penny. It was a pure commission plus renewal opportunity. No salary.

Since we were in a financial downturn, I took on this challenge full steam ahead. I had a goal of getting rid of my student loans as quickly as possible. I had no idea how I was going to accomplish this, but I made it a priority. This is truly the biggest obstacle for people about money – making it a priority.

By the time I was 24, I realized that I was paying 6, 7 and 8% in interest on these loans. It was absurd. Back then, I had quarterly bonuses, so I used those monies to pay off my student loans – chunks at a time. Would I much rather have liked to go on vacation with that money? Absolutely. Would I rather have put that money into my 401(k)? Without a doubt. But getting rid of that debt really gave me a sense of freedom. That was my only debt at that time, so it was a huge burden off of my shoulders.

Fast forward to age 26. I finally finished paying off $54,000 in student loans. It took me four years. It was not pretty, but I was able to get it done. I celebrate this every year with a nice glass of wine. In my calendar, I keep score by having a reminder pop up on March 30th that I paid off my student loans. Keeping score can be fun, too!

Now that I am 34, I would have done things so much differently when I was younger. I would have saved so much more. But back then, I didn't have proper habits. I didn't keep score. I was the one GIVING the financial advice. didn't spend a lot of time on my own finances because I did not have a plan and I did not keep score.

Writing down my spending habits makes me think twice before spending money. Especially on things that I do not need.

My focus right now is to put away and invest as much money as I possibly can while giving my family a comfortable lifestyle. My mindset has absolutely changed. When I was younger, I thought that you needed a nice watch or car to be successful. There are people who have nice things but have very little savings or investments. Looking rich is a lot more popular than actually being rich these days. And I like nice things, but there is a time and place for them.

I'd much rather invest money right now for long-term compounding growth potential rather than buy something that is unnecessary.

That isn't the case for most people. I've learned this habit by reading other financial books. I've learned from others, since our educational system fails us with the education of money. As a Financial Advisor, I often feel like I am a wealth coach, therapist and preserver. I wear a lot of hats.

Reading this book can help you get ahead on your financial journey. And when you pay attention to your pennies, your pennies have the potential to make dollars. Dollars can turn into hundreds. Hundreds to thousands. You get the picture. It all comes down to making a choice to want to get ahead. As the great professional writer Benjamin Hardy said in the title of his book, *Willpower Doesn't Work*. I was given this book at my Strategic Coach class and boy did it open my mind.

We all say we want to be rich. Wealthy. Have more time on our hands, have more luxuries. But getting to that point is extremely difficult.

Automation is your friend!

I think the reason people don't save money is because they do not automate their processes. When people receive their paycheck, they usually pay their bills, credit card and debts first. They are left with little after their expenses. THIS is the reason why people don't get ahead. They burden themselves with unnecessary liabilities so that they cannot get out of the proverbial rat race.

If you automatically had 20% of your check go into savings and investments, you would be forced to spend less. It would motivate you to earn more money and do better if you wanted more things. Again, things don't make you rich, but you need a balance in your life, too.

Automate money to go into your 401(k). Automate money to go into an investment account. Learn about the stock market. Keep score of how well your money does and where it goes.

Only by keeping score, will you see improvements in your finances.

Here is a fun exercise. Take out a calculator and add up all of the money that you spent on your credit card in the past 30 days. I bet that you will be shocked. I was when I recently did this. Absolutely shocked. I am investing a lot of money in my business at the moment, so it definitely opened my eyes to my own spending.

I'm spending on investments. People are buying liabilities. Again, that Gucci shirt that was $500 will not bring you a return on your money. Again, this all comes down to financial education.

The biggest pieces of advice that I can give beginners are the following:

1. **Write down every single penny that you spend. Make it a habit.** Be aware of what you're doing. Don't be a zombie with your money.

2. **Make a plan. Have a savings goal.** Have an investment goal. Work with someone if you don't know how to do this.

3. **Have your investing and saving done automatically.** Make it as simple as possible for you to get ahead.

4. If you want to save a certain amount of money, use a time value of money calculator to show you how much you need to save to reach your goal. (If you want to save x amount of dollars, it is easy to find a "time value of money" calculator to show you how much you need to save each month.)

Consistency
"Never wish life were easier, wish that you were better. It's really simple . . . If you want life to change, you have to change. If you want life to get better, you have to get better. Success is nothing more than a few simple disciplines, practiced every day."
–Jim Rohn

Consistency is the key. Consistency is one of, if not, the most critical aspect of our lives. Taking care of yourself, eating well, working out, your money and happiness is all about your daily habits. Your daily choices/habits add up to your week, your month, your year and build/or subtract from your retirement/future.

I preach this to my clients. I preach this to myself. This is not something that you or I will perfect in a day, a week or a month. So, don't get discouraged. I, too, go through times when consistency is difficult.

Things come up in life. Family issues, work issues and the list could go on and on. But when you put structure in your life, magical things start to happen.

Being consistent has allowed me to become financially free at the age of 34. Income exceeds debts, monthly, with recurring revenue. That is the basic definition of being financially retired.

As my mentor and coach, Dan Sullivan says, "Retirement is for machines." He believes that retirement is not for humans. We need to have a purpose and a drive to live. **When you stop working, you tend to stop living with a purpose or a consistent message.**

Having a purpose all comes down to what you want. I love Dan's Book, *Wanting What You Want*. That has been a favorite of mine for years. It is okay to want nice things. I recommend that you have a plan in place to get them. If you have a plan, you can be consistent. When you are consistent, you can achieve your goals faster.

When you want to start a new workout routine or a meal plan, start small. Yes, you read that right. Small. Make it easy and make it fun for yourself.

If you want to go to the gym, go once a week. But do this for four weeks in a row. Then after that, add a day for another four weeks. Then three times a week. Get the idea?

The same is true for your money. It is quite difficult to say to yourself "today, I will have all my finances in order!" It does not work like that. You need to set up a plan to get into financial shape. And the plan needs to be consistent; taking one simple step at a time.

Be patient with yourself. It is okay to go slow. It all starts with writing down your spending. In order to get ahead, writing down your daily spending will be your starting point. Use the Money Journal in this book to help you with this process.

As best-selling author and financial coach Marlene Elizabeth says, "Transformation takes *time*. My biggest piece of advice for you is don't wait to unfold your financial dream. Take action now. Don't let this opportunity slip through your fingers. Choose one mini action step you can take in the next 5 seconds and keep going."

If you are reading this book and you are just starting out in the work force or are still in school, this is amazing. You are already on your way to a bright financial future. Start getting into this consistent habit of writing down your spending. Write down your goals. Write down how much money you would like to have when you are 30, 40, 50 and so on. This will trigger your brain to start thinking about ways to accomplish these goals. Get ready for amazing things to start happening.

If you are in the middle of your working career, this book will help you regain that financial confidence and can help you get back on course for your future retirement. If you start paying attention to your dollars, you could pay down debt faster, have no mortgage and possibly retire earlier if you invest well. Who doesn't want more time to enjoy their life?

Having awareness of where your money is going/ your spending on a daily basis allows you to start to make choices on how to spend/invest future dollars. Once you know where you are at, you can choose how you want to move forward.

Lastly, I love retirees. They are my favorite group of clients to work with. This book can help you re-focus your spending in retirement. That is one thing that you can control – your spending. When you want to retire, you need to know what your fixed expenses will be every month. When you know this number, you are able to plan on receiving income from your investments every month in retirement. It all comes down to having consistent spending habits and knowing where you are at. Starting with an emergency fund or a cash reserve is a great way to begin. By tracking your daily spending, you are going to start seeing patterns. These patterns will show you where your money is going. And then you can ask yourself if you really need to be spending money on these items, things or food.

Instead of buying a $5 coffee every day, save that money. You could put $25 a week into your savings account. That $25 will quickly turn into $100. That

$100 then turns into $1,200 a year. That is real money. "Found Money."

When you accurately write down what you are spending your money on daily and how much it is costing you, it will be obvious where you could cut back spending and save or invest those dollars instead.

Starting to notice your overspending starts by writing down all of the items you buy. Everything. By cutting these spending habits out of your life, you could consistently save money, invest more money and be in a better financial situation. It is truly not that difficult to get a hold of your financial life. It all starts with a choice. The choice to write down your spending.

Every single day.

By being consistent, you could start a savings and investing plan. Here's an idea. When we look back to the $5 coffee a day habit, let's say that you stop doing that and save that money. That is the start. You set a goal to save and invest that money every month. Half of the money goes into savings and the other half goes into investments. Do you think this could help you have a better financial future rather than buying your daily mocha-choca latte? It most likely will help you have a better financial future.

Being consistent all starts with a choice. A choice of wanting to be better. To get better with your money. The desire to make better decisions with your money. Write down your purchases.

Let's look at an example. We have a 35-year-old that wants to buy a $1,000 watch. A fancy watch. This 35-year-old makes $20 an hour before taxes. He has had his eye on this watch for a couple of years now. In order for him to buy this watch, do you know how many hours he will have to spend at work to make it happen? He is going to have to work at least 50 hours to make the dream watch his.

Another option could be him buying the watch on his credit card now, and he could pay it off in a month or two. Instant gratification. This is the choice that a lot of people would make. Just buy it now and pay it off when I can because I know that I have a paycheck coming in two weeks. Do you think he is making consistent wise choices with his money with this mindset? Probably not. Perhaps there is a great watch he would almost be happy with for a smaller purchase price? It's good to stop and check in and see if this makes sense in your financial plan. And if you don't have a financial plan, you should get one! By checking in, you are not just buying and paying it off when you can, you are actually going to see if your purchase fits your financial plan.

And when you look at this example, this is not including the taxes that he has to pay on his 50 hours of work. In reality, it will take more than a week's worth of work to pay for an item that is not needed. Remember, you can't get your time back. Once it is gone, it is gone. So why let your instant gratification habit hamper your future?

To simplify this concept even further, if you earned $20 an hour and worked 40 hours in a week (not adding in taxes etc.) that means you're earning $800 a week. So, it would take over a week to earn the $1,000 for the watch. Plus, you may have additional expenses to think about too. Here is another way you could still work toward your watch, not go into debt and build for your future:

Of the $800 a week you earn ...

Put $250 a week toward your watch.

Put $350 toward your weekly expenses.

Put $100 a week toward your savings/emergency fund.

Put $100 a week toward your future/retirement.

At the end of one month you would have:

$1,000 for your watch AND

$400 toward your emergency fund/unexpected expenses AND

$400 to invest toward your future AND

Would have been able to pay $1,400 toward monthly expenses like food, gas, rent, etc. AND

No debt to worry about as you enjoy your watch and build toward your future! J

There are better ways to get what you want and still plan for a better financial future. When you consistently stop and think about your purchases and if they will help you in your future, you will create a different mindset for your money.

Here is another way to work for this watch. Let your money work for you. Don't you think it would be better to invest $200 a month and be patient by allowing for potential gains from your investments to pay for your watch? Well, here is how that could work.

You could invest $200 a month from your paycheck instead of spending it. If you invest your money, you now have the opportunity to let that money potentially grow. Your watch is not going anywhere, but your investment account IS going somewhere. Hopefully it is going up in value.

Then, the next month you invest another $200. Then the month after that, another $200. You could let time be your friend here. Hopefully, over time, your account appreciates, you could use your GAINS to pay for your watch instead of your paycheck.

You see, you are starting a good habit here. You are beginning to let your money work for you, instead of you always working for money. When you consistently have this mentality, you will begin to look at things differently. Your spending habits will look different. Consistency with your positive habits are designed to give you a new outlook on money. Those spontaneous purchases will start to slow down.

Going back to our watch, there are so many ways that you could make it happen. You could possibly still have the $1,000 in your investment account, instead of your credit card bill. You now have your new watch and you are still being consistent by investing money on a monthly basis. This option and opportunity are better for your long-term financial health. Realizing the power of compounding interest could help you see a bigger fortune for your future.

It all comes down to being aware, consistent and making choices for your short-term and long-term goals. Every month, utilize your extra savings by investing, while letting the potential growth pay for the items that you want over time. The more aware you are of your money, the potential for an early retirement could become reality.

You can automate all of this, too. You can make life very easy for yourself. Every month you should know where you are making money and where it is going. Plain and simple. Be consistent with the additional money every month and work for a bigger and better financial future.

By automating that $200 withdrawal from your bank account to your investment account, you take the thinking out of the picture. You could also automatically buy investments that you want to help grow your money. Take the thinking out of the equation. You can automatically buy investments every month and not have to think about it. This is truly being consistent.

The same goes for your savings account. The days that you get paid, you could automatically have money put into your savings account. Take the thinking and action out of the picture. Let technology and time work for you!

CONSISTENT MONEY SUCCESS TIPS

1. Track your spending.

2. Resist impulse buying. Instead make a short-term plan (1 to 3 months) to achieve your purchasing goal while building toward your future.

3. Remember to consistently build toward your future.

4. Lean into automation to support you in being consistent.

KEEPING IT SIMPLE

Most people are going to think that it is difficult to write down their spending. That's true. It is not easy. I, too, struggle with it some days. However, I choose to build the powerful habit of tracking what I spend. It takes consistency, diligence and commitment.

But then again, most things that are good do not come easy to us. **Success comes from creating amazing habits.** This is a lifetime thing. Success does not come overnight. Writing your spending down is a transformational habit that can help you toward financial success.

If you think this will be hard, well, I'm here to make it easy for you. I've even created a money tracking tool that can help you called: The Money Journal. (You can find it on Amazon.)

This truly only takes a few moments of your day. This will take less time to complete than the time we spend on social media and our emails.

The reality of this is to start to become aware of what you're doing. Every day. When you write down your spending habits, you become more aware of what you're actually doing. This is the key.

Once you are aware, you can continue your current spending habits or choose to shift your spending to be more in alignment with your current and future goals.

Let's create a plan to get you into better spending habits. Your better habits can create new opportunities for you to have a better financial future. A better financial future can lead to more time to enjoy your life as you wish. Who doesn't want that?

Okay, here we go. Remember, we want to keep things simple.

Let's pick one day. Just one.

Start out by writing out your spending and expenses for one full day. Just do one day. Use your journal. Take it with you, from the morning until night.

This exercise will make you not only mindful of you having this journal on you, but it will make you mindful as to where your money is going and what form of payment you are using.

This is the key. Start becoming aware. Be mindful. Be educated.

Remember, you deserve to have your money go where you want it to, not to other companies that are not benefiting YOU!

So, we are going to do a full day's worth of spending. Just one. It is not that bad or hard. Believe me, I've done it plenty of times. When you buy your morning coffee and muffin, write it down. If you buy something on the internet, write it down. Complete this task for one day. At the end of the day, review your purchases.

What are your purchases telling you from the first day? What is your brain telling you? I bet that you are already connecting the dots as to why you are writing down your spending.

Now that you have one day completed, schedule a day the following week to do this again. Pick a day, put it in your calendar and do it.

It is simple. Consciously make the decision to do this exercise again.

Throughout the day, morning through night, write down in your journal everything that you spend money on. At night, review your transactions. **Start becoming aware about your money.**

Now that you have done this twice in two weeks, what are your purchases telling you? Are you seeing any habits, just after two days? I'd guess that the answer is yes, but everyone is different.

Congratulate yourself. You have now spent two days of your life making a positive difference toward your financial future. You may not see it yet, but you are on a great path.

I bet you know what is next! Choose a day the following week to do the same thing. You're going to start a habit without even realizing it.

Start small. Start slow. Start making this part of your thinking. This is how you win. Winning is good.

So, after the first month, you should have AT LEAST four days that you kept track of your spending. This is a HUGE accomplishment. Congratulations!

I'd advise you to write down in your Money Journal what your thoughts are on your spending. What are you realizing? What are you consistently spending money on? What are you grateful for?

Your Money Journal is going to become your new best friend. Your future self will thank you later!

Month #2!

Now that you have gone through your first four days of your Money Journal entries, let's kick things up a notch.

For each week in month two, schedule two days a week for you to bring your journal with you everywhere and write down what you are spending money on. It is just two days a week at this point. This does not disrupt your day. This is just an opportunity for you to be better with your hard-earned dollars.

Complete two days a week, each week, for the second month. If you feel inclined to do more, do it. That will help you create your better habits faster.

Now that you are doing your Money Journal entries two days a week, you are creating a muscle memory for your brain. You brain may be telling you to bring your journal with you more often. If that is the case, please do so. If you feel inclined to do more, please do so. You are in control here. It would be amazing for you to increase the number of days that you are using your Money Journal.

Month #3!

Yep, you guessed it! You are going to bring your Money Journal with you three days a week, every week, in the third month. There is a reasoning behind this. You are slowly allowing your brain to get used to this new habit. Your new habit will be a fun habit, because you are doing something to help yourself, and who doesn't want to help themselves?

The biggest opportunity to win with this is to plan on using your Money Journal. Picking which days over the first couple months will help you get into a rhythm. This rhythm will build momentum in your brain to remember to do this.

If you leave your Money Journal at home on accident, don't get upset or disappointed. You can always write your spending down throughout the day. Believe me, I've had to do that before. It is not a big deal. The main thing here is to be consistent.

By the time you get to month three, you are going to be on a roll. You're going to be so much more aware. You will know and see your spending habits. Your brain is not developing a new muscle to show you how to make progress on your financial future.

If you are spending money on lunch, as an example, every day, you can see how much this is costing you. When you add up your spending on lunches per week, you can see how much that is holding you back. After one month of you writing things down in your Money Journal, you will see how much you have spent on lunches throughout the month. Then you can simply multiply that number by 12 to see what lunches are approximately costing you a year. I bet you are going to be surprised by the figure that you see.

This will be an "Ah ha!" moment for you. This can be true of ordering take out. Coffee runs. Clothes. The list goes on and on. These are just the simple ones that most people do on a daily or weekly basis.

Here is the real kicker. When you use the principals in this book, you will realize that the money you're spending on these items could be used to pursue an early retirement, a bigger investment account or a possible better financial future. It is very powerful to see how much money you could have in the future when you compound your money in investments instead of spending it.

Month #4

By the fourth month, you will most likely be bringing your Money Journal with you daily. You are building up this habit over time.

Trying to do this every day right away will be hard. Most likely too hard to make it sustainable. This is why I'm setting up a process for you to follow. A process that will allow you to really understand where your money is going. Every day you will begin to start making different money decisions. Decisions such as, "Do I really need this?" Or, "Should I buy this?"

"Will this help my future financial self?"

If you have to ask yourself those questions, you probably don't need it. This is all part of your brain working FOR you. Helping you.

Each day that you bring your Money Journal with you, you are doing yourself a favor. You are helping yourself.

Imagine yourself one year from now, and you have a daily habit of writing down your spending . . . Envision how much money you could save yourself. **How much money you could invest instead of spending it? How much debt you could FINALLY get rid of by being knowledgeable as to where your money is going. Your financial life is about to change forever!**

The Simple Process:

1st Month – 1x a week – total of four days this month

2nd Month – 2x a week – total of eight days this month

3rd Month – 3x a week – total of 12 days this month

4th Month – You should be able to really dial this in and start doing this daily.

Building this powerful habit will help you create great awareness of where your dollars are going. Discovering where your money is going will then give you the choice to continue to spend as you are or perhaps shift to align more powerfully with your short-term and long-term goals. This will help you reduce debt, increase savings and build a powerful and positive relationship with your money.

KEEPING IT SIMPLE TIPS

1. Start tracking your spending.

2. Start slowly and build the habit and awareness of tracking your spending.

3. Each day you track, spend some time at the end of the day reflecting on what you're discovering about your spending.

4. Build up to tracking three days a week.

5. Apply the information and insights you are discovering about your spending and look at how you can align future spending more closely with your current and long-term goals.

6. Celebrate building a more powerful and connected relationship with your money.

7. Remember—keep it simple. J

BYE-BYE DEBT

"You must gain control over your money
because if you don't,
it will forever control you."
--Bill Bloom

I'm going to help you learn about debt in this chapter.

Debt is usually the Achilles heel of finances. Time after time I have seen people with too much debt.

We are constantly bombarded with offers. 0% financing for 60 months. We will pay your first payment. The ads go on and on and on. Debt is easy to apply for and build. But as it builds, it starts to take over and control us. It is far easier to build debt than it is to pay it off.

I think you get my point. We are controlled by debt.

Yet, as easy as it is to get into debt, I don't believe enough is being done to teach people how to get out of debt. Later in this chapter, I give you some strategies to help you get out of debt.

When you took business classes in school, if you took them, did they ever teach you how to get out of debt?

Was there a class on eliminating debt in high school or college?

The answer is obviously no.

When I spoke about how a mortgage works in a previous chapter, I bet that was an eye-opener for you, as it was for me when I actually looked at my mortgage.

I couldn't believe that I could buy another property with the interest that I would be paying over 30 years. It was an eye-opening experience.

That is just one example of how debt doesn't help you.

What about buying furniture with debt? Lots of times companies will offer 0% financing for 36 or 60 months. These offers seem harmless, but they are a trap.

A trap on your monthly cash flow.

Let's pretend that you just moved into a new home. Congratulations! It is truly amazing to have a home. Know how much it will truly cost you.

You head out to a furniture store; they offer you 0% financing for 36 months. When you get that offer, do you think you're going to end up spending more than what you planned on? Most likely.

You see, we as humans have a hard time saying no to offers like these. We think, it's 0%! That's an amazing deal. But what you don't realize is that this could cost you over time.

Let me explain.

You spend $15,000 on new furniture for your beautiful new home. You originally planned on spending only $5,000. That is a big increase. You're all excited and are now making emotional decisions.

You're not going to have a monthly payment. A payment that you could be investing instead and making money for yourself.

You see, when you know where your dollars are going, you don't have to rely on these offers and end up spending more money than you planned.

In this example, the $15,000 debt will create a $416.67 monthly payment for you. That could really affect your monthly cash flow situation if you don't plan properly.

Would you rather be paying the furniture company $416.67 a month or yourself that same amount of money? Think about that next time you want to take out debt.

If you have debt, I'm going to explain some tips for you to get out of your debt.

I've seen debt cripple people's financial lives. That in turn boils over into their personal lives. It's not pretty.

If you have mortgage, credit card payments, a car payment and student loans, this could really hamper your ability to invest. I was in this situation when I graduated college. I had over $54,000 of student loans when I graduated. That was a lot of money. Playing soccer in college paid for half of my tuition. All of those long hours on the practice fields paid off. I'd say that was a good investment!

I paid off my student loans in 3 years after college. I looked at the interest payments that I had to make, and they were very high! My student loans had a 5, 6 and 7% interest on my loans. Let me remind you, I had no salary from my business at that time. I had to go out and make things happen to make money. If I did not go out and see prospect and clients, I was not making a penny. This was really hard for me, but it was a goal that I wanted to achieve.

Remember, believing is key!

Here's what I did. I looked at my highest percentage of interest on my loans, and decided to aggressively pay those off first. When I completed one, I aggressively went onto the next highest interest payment. Then I went to the next one when that was finished.

7 percent then 6 percent and then 5 . . . I think you get the idea.

Let's continue. Write out all of your debts. Create a spreadsheet, hire a financial advisor or work with your accountant on this project. If you don't understand how numbers work, hire a professional! You could see greater results faster with their help.

Write down the total amount of debt you owe in one column. Then, write down the interest rate that you are paying. Next, write down your monthly payments.

Seeing this on paper will be eye-opening. You will visualize how much money you're spending, what interest percentages you're paying and the total amount of debt that you are in!

Lastly, ask yourself if any of these debts are helping you financially. The answer is probably an astounding NO!

So, let's say you have a credit card payment that has a 25% APR interest payment, student loans at 5%, a car payment at 4% and a mortgage at 3.5%.

From my own personal example above, I went after the highest payment if interest first. So, for this example, we should work to get rid of your credit card payment first. Paying 25% interest is hard to get out from under. It is difficult to make that kind of return in the stock market.

Focus on paying off your credit card debt. Make it a priority. Make it a goal. And when you reach a goal, reward yourself. Think of something that you would like to do to reward yourself for eliminating your credit card debt.

You can make this fun for yourself. Make it a game. Have fun with it. You're going to be better off when your debt is gone, so make it a mission to get rid of it!

After your credit card debt is gone, stop using your credit card, unless it is an emergency! It is crucial not to fall back into bad habits. Put the credit cards away and out of your wallet except for one. That one should be used for emergencies only.

Next, in my example, you will want to eliminate your student loan debt! Educational loans can be a great investment if used properly. It can help you advance in life and in your specific fields of work. Now that you're making money, it is time to get rid of your student loans.

I'm going to share a neat trick with you to get rid of debt faster. Remember how you had your monthly credit card payments? Well, let's say you had a $500 a month credit card payment and now those payments are gone! Congratulations! Here's what you want to do next . . . put that extra $500 a month toward your student loan payments. Yes, snowball your payments. It will help you pay down your student loans faster.

This is the key. Snowballing your payments will help you focus your attention as to where your money is actually going.

By eliminating debt, you can start to free up monthly cash flow. Keep paying down your debts, don't fall back into bad habits and focus on growing your wealth.

The next payment on your list will be your car payment, then your mortgage. **By eliminating this debt, you have increased your monthly cash flow to invest which could create a bigger and better future for yourself!**

If you hired a financial advisor to help you with your debt elimination, ask them to help you invest that extra monthly cash flow. Start striving to make money with your money. Let it work for you! Instead of giving it to other companies to make money on your money. It is yours! Treat it well.

As my friend and fellow entrepreneur Jon LeDuca told me, "I try to put mine (money) to good use and to dream about ways money can be applied in my life. It's a tool for manifesting my dreams."

Money is a tool. He is right about that. Don't let money control you. Control what you do WITH your money and where it goes.

At the end of the day, it is your choice where your money goes. Choose wisely!

BYE-BYE DEBT TIPS

1. It is easier to get into debt than out of (so avoid creating debt as much as possible).

2. Know that you can pay off your debt.

3. Make a get out of debt a goal and build a plan to do so.

4. Believe in yourself! You can do it!

5. Reward yourself as you make progress.

6. As you pay off your debt, stop using your credit cards.

7. Start having your money go toward your goals. Enjoy the increased cash flow and invest in your future.

PROGRESS, NOT PERFECTION

Progress is the key to great things in life.

In today's world, we get caught up in making things perfect. Perfect life, perfect picture, perfect car, perfect home and the list goes on. But let's face it. Perfection is an opinion. And when it comes to your money, it is more important to make progress with your financial decisions than to wait to make the perfect decision.

Perfection is not a thing. Progress is.

You see, when you make progress, it makes you happier. Every day, when you accomplish something, it does have an impact on your brain and body. Tony Robbins is a huge believer in making progress. He states that in order to be happy, you MUST make progress. That is the secret to happiness. Progress.

Dan Sullivan, the man behind Strategic Coach, says that in order to move forward, you need to make progress, not perfection. Most of the time, 80% completion is going to be good enough. And if you need the other 20% done, delegate those activities to others who have special unique abilities to complete the task.

These two legends have a great take on life. They both have different yet fantastic points of views on life and happiness.

Money plays a big part in our lives. Some people's happiness is tied to how positive a money situation they are in. This is true for most people. When you are not doing well financially, that stress becomes a huge burden in your life. And it remains there until you dig your way out of your financial distress. When you are in a positive money situation with a plan for your retirement, it creates ease and gives you peace and confidence.

For some people, they never get out of financial distress. Their habits really weigh them down and they don't realize that they are the problem. It's not the economy, it's not the government, it's not the post office. It is them. They want to blame everyone else for the mistakes that they are making. The truth is, they need to wake up and realize that they can be in control of their financial lives. We have the ability to make that happen. It all starts with a choice.

Jim Rohn got himself into a better financial position, quickly and at a young age, by realizing that all of these entities were not the reason that he was broke. He was the reason!

By having this epiphany, he started to make better financial decisions on a daily basis. He was making PROGRESS. At one point in his life, he consolidated all of his smaller loans into one large hard to pay loan and this really buried him financially. Once he made the decision to stop the harassing collection calls, he took the money into the collection agency and threw it all over the agency's desk! That was a WOW moment for Jim. He finally got out of his own way and started his journey to financial freedom.

At that time, he was a husband and a father. This was a big motivating factor for him to change his ways. By making progress in a side business that he started, it allowed him to match the amount of money that he was making at his full-time job. In only six months. How amazing is that!

And after 12 months, he doubled what he was making at this full-time job with his new side business. That truly gave him the flexibility to make progress. He didn't strive for perfection. He strove to make progress. Every single day. If you want to learn more about his story, Go here: https://www.youtube.com/watch?v=arUini9Mh6A.

In today's world, we have so much information directly at our fingertips. Between our smart phones, tablets, computers, the news and television, you could really learn anything. To better yourself financially, you could read a book such as this one. You can send this book to five of your friends who truly need financial help. You could take a class on personal finance to learn more about creating a better future.

We really and truly have an abundance of resources to educate ourselves. There are countless YouTube videos, books, webinars and in person seminars where you can learn to make better financial decisions. And by buying and reading this book, you are already making PROGRESS.

This is why striving for perfection could be damaging to your financial future. I've spoken with people who have held their money in a safe savings account at the bank, waiting for the next depression to invest their money. By taking this approach, this person waited for the perfect time to invest, but there is never a perfect time to invest. What we have to look at is now. How can we make progress toward your goals?

Are there better times than others? Yes, but we don't know what the future holds. That's why you need to make progress and come up with a plan that is encompassed around your goals. Hiring a professional to help you with his could help, too!

In my life, I've had obstacles to overcome as well. When I graduated college, I had over $54,000 of student loan debt. That is a lot of money. When I started working, I didn't have a salary! I had to create my own! That was incredibly tough being a 22-year-old with no income and all of this debt. But I said to myself, I am going to figure this out.

My goal was to get rid of my student loan debt as quickly as possible. It took me a couple of years to do this, but I was able to achieve this goal because I made progress toward the goals. When I received my quarterly bonuses, I would not spend them. I would pay off my student loan debt with them. If I had a good month at work and made more money, I would pay off more than I normally would on my student loans. I made progress. I tried to make progress on them every day, week and month. That focus helped me get out of student loan debt in less than three years.

That was such a gift. Not only because of the progress that I was making, but because of the work ethic that I created. I worked harder than smarter to get to my goals. I was able to help others with their financial lives because I was so motivated to do better for others. And in turn, I did better, too. It was, and still is to this day, an unbelievable experience that has helped equip me to help others.

My passion gave me the opportunity to make progress. I chose to do this. I chose to make it happen. It all comes down to our choices. The same could be said about Jim Rohn and the choices that he made throughout his career. These decisions to set a goal, keep track of your progress, not focusing on perfection and actually going out there and doing it is what it is all about. By paying off my student loans, I taught myself how to manage my money. And I still did not have a salary. I had to go out create it every day. That is the life of an entrepreneur. Not everyone is cut out for that, but it really made me think about money in a different light. And now I get to teach others about the lessons that I learned about money.

The reason why I am telling you all of this is because you can get control of your financial life. It all starts with a choice. Our Money Journal was created to help you plan a better financial future. As was this book. I wanted to empower you to be a better you. Money is so emotional and you can have a better sense of where you are going with a financial plan.

When you learn about your spending habits, you can change them. But in order to do so, you absolutely need to be aware of them. Writing down your spending will open your eyes as to where your money is really going. Take the time to use the Money Journal to learn about your spending habits. Write down your spending, see where your money is going, reposition where your money needs to go in order for you to pursue your financial goals!

You can do this. Just take one step, one choice at a time and make consistent progress toward your goals.

PROGRESS, NOT PERFECTION TIPS

1. Release perfection as a goal.

2. What financial goal are you wanting to make progress on?

3. Start to track your spending and progress towards our goal(s)? (The Money Journal can help you do this.)

4. Adjust habits to help you make progress toward your goal(s).

5. You can do this! One step, one choice at a time. Remember, progress, not perfection.

THE WAY TO GAIN CONTROL OF YOUR MONEY

"Don't be afraid to give up the good to go for the great."
--John D. Rockefeller

Money is a fictitious thing. Money has become a fictional means to an end. The purposeful use of physical denominations of dollars has drastically disappeared over the past 10 years.

Ask yourself, when is the last time that you used physical cash to pay for something? Going to a bank or an ATM has become a thing of the past. It is so incredibly easy to take out your wallet, pay for a $5 cup of coffee and go about your day. I see it every day here in downtown Chicago. People spending countless dollars on their coffees, lunches, after hour drinks and dinners. If you work a 60-hour work week, you have only 108 hours left in your week to yourself. People want to have fun during this time. Your sleep will reduce your number of available hours a week. After getting your 8 hours of sleep each night, you're left with 52 hours to do what you want. This is where you're spending comes into play. As humans, we want to be entertained. Buying the $5 coffee is a habit that is fun for you, for the moment. This goes into how you pay for your coffee or lunch. You probably pull out your debit or credit card and spend. Spend, spend, spend. **Humans are definitely good at spending! Wouldn't you agree?**

Amazon, online shopping, sales, door busters and the list goes on and on and on. Retailers want your information, primarily your email, to send you fun offers that make you feel good. Buy this at 30% off! But you must buy it before X date. **Urgency. This is your money's worst friend.** You have to buy this before the sale runs out! Oh, Oh Oh I want it. How many sweaters do you really need? How many pairs of shoes do you really need? Your mind automatically goes into happy mode – endorphins, temporary happiness – so you go online and buy that purple sweater that you don't need. Then, the package shows up at your doorstep! Fantastic! You did not have to even leave your house! Take a moment to think about this. After you open your package, take that purple sweater out of the wrapping, how do you really feel? Regret? Remorse? Do you ever think to yourself, "Why did I even buy this?"

I think this happens a lot. We as humans get caught up in the moment. Companies create urgency. They create sales. Buying something on sale still means you part ways with your hard-earned money. I know the answer to this already, but I'm going to ask the question anyways to get you thinking. How much time did it take you to earn money to pay for your purple sweater?

Pause. Hm . . . I really don't know! The majority of people don't know the value of their time. They don't know how much time they need to work to pay for that sweater. If you knew that it would take you 4 hours of your workday to pay for that item, would you reconsider? Would you think twice about buying things? Maybe it could help you start to realize where your money is actually going. Breaking down your after-tax dollars by hours worked can give you your hourly rate. Let's look at an example. You make $50,000 after taxes, benefits and investing in your company's 401(k) plan. Great. That is a good number to figure for your own financial situation. Next, you have your hours that you work each week. Let's use 50 hours a week. 50 hours multiplied by 48 weeks, assuming 4 weeks of vacation time, will give you 2,400 hours worked for the year. $50,000 divided by 2,400 hours will give you an after-tax hourly wage of 20.83 dollars an hour.

Now, let's use that sweater. Assume it was $100. It will take you 5 hours to buy that item. Is it worth five hours of your time?

Housing. Let's look at an even bigger expense. The average rent in the city of Chicago is $1,882.92. (https://www.numbeo.com/cost-of-living/in/Chicago)

That is for a one-bedroom apartment. If we go back to our earlier math, $1,882.92 divided by $20.83 means you need to work 90.39 hours to pay your monthly rent. Wowzah, that's a lot of time. Almost half of your time working each month goes toward having a roof over your head. If you make less money, then you are absolutely affected more than someone who is a higher earner. The moral of the story is that you need to know your hourly value. This is so important for you to understand. When you go out on the weekends and spend frivolously, you don't have an understanding as to the financial impact that this will have on your life. You do not know the time value of those dollars that just disappeared out of your pocket. Where does it all go? No wonder people have a hard time saving. I have heard people say that they don't have any money left over at the end of the month. Where did it all go, I'll ask, and most of the time people have no clue. **This is the problem. When you cannot keep track or understand where your money is going, you don't have a great chance to get ahead in life.** Yes, sometimes you can catch a break and inherit monies or sell something for a profit, but most of the time those monies will disappear due to your poor money habits. Where does your money go? You don't know. What happens when you have a financial emergency? You don't have savings to pay for it. Then you go into debt to pay for that emergency. Credit cards. A loan. Interest. You're now behind. This is an issue.

Throughout life we are going to have expenses. But you are in control of where you live, where you spend your money and where your money goes.

This is why writing down your spending is so important. The Money Journal helps you take control of your spending. A lot of our spending problems could be fixed by keeping track. Don't be afraid to jump in and start keeping track. Your financial future awaits greatness!

TIPS TO GAIN CONTROL

1. Figure out your hourly rate.
2. Pause before spending and calculate the hourly cost.
3. Track your cash flow.
4. Choose to spend on what is in alignment with your goals.

RETIRE AS YOU DESIRE

"Income that lasts one's lifetime is the key to a bountiful retirement."
--Bill Bloom

Time.

Time is our most valuable commodity.

Here in America, retirement is part of the American Dream.

Retirement planning is THE part of my business that I love the most.

Unfortunately, I find, most people do not understand how to actually retire and struggle with how to be able to retire with confidence. There are so many tools, resources, products and experts that are available to support you. Yet we don't always know where to start. The good news is that you don't have to figure it out on your own. Remember you can get the support and help of an expert to help you leverage the time you have most powerfully.

Perhaps that is because we live such work-focused lives. We focus on today's actions. It is hard to visualize what your future will look like in 20, 30 or 40 years from now.

Starting to invest and save for your retirement is so much harder beginning at 50 as opposed to 35.

You see, time is on the side of the 35-year-old. The 35-year-old is going to have the potential to compound his or her investments over time more so than the 50-year-old.

When you are young, take advantage of time. Your financial future could depend on it.

Here's another thing, you don't need to work until 65 to retire . . .

In order to Retire As You Desire, you really need to get your financials in order. You need to get your cash flow in order. But the thing is, you don't have to wait until you are 65 to do this. Now is the time. Not "someday."

The sooner you realize your daily money habits, the sooner you could be on your way to financial freedom. What if you could build daily money habits that would support you both now and in the future? Everyday building toward a more and more powerful future.

What if you had less debt? Possibly no debt. How would it make you feel if you had no mortgage? No car payment? No Credit Card bills?

I'd venture to say that you would be pretty happy with that extra money every month both for today and the future. When you have time on your side, you can make a plan to eliminate debt. Save more money. Invest more money. You could compound your investments in a more productive manner when you start early.

If you have a goal, you could make them happen when you have a plan for how your money will be used. The sooner you start the sooner you can start building toward your future.

When you get into your 60's and you haven't spent much time planning for your retirement, it gets so much harder to live the life of your dreams. There are a lot of reasons why this makes life more difficult.

Compounding interest is the first one. If your money is growing over time, it compounds. It gets bigger. This is such a crucial part to investing. Starting to save for retirement at 60 makes life difficult. There is a probability that you will have to continue working, depending on how much debt you have.

Imagine not saving enough or still having a large amount of debt going into retirement. That doesn't sound like much fun. It sounds like working until you cannot work any longer is going to be your best option.

However, the 35-year-old that started saving early and put a plan together for their money would have a better chance of retiring on their terms since they know where their money is going.

You see, this is the difference between living the financial life that you want and being part of the "rat race" mentality that exists here in America.

The "rat race" mentality states that you should work from 18 or 22, depending on whether you went to college or not, and work until 65 by getting a "good job" and work your way up the corporate ladder. But imagine if you retired at age 65 and got ill at 68. You may not have the retirement of your dreams. You may not enjoy your retirement at all if you become sick.

This is why I am encouraging you to start planning early. When you run out of time to work and save money, it is very difficult to live comfortably in your later years in life.

I've witnessed this firsthand. It's not pretty.

When I first started in the financial world in 2008, I realized that people were making emotional decisions with their money because of the stock market drop. Fear really hurt many people's investments during that time. They didn't think that their money would recover. As we all know, the stock market did recover during that time.

This time period really made me think. It allowed me to think about how to help people. I really got a chance to learn from people's mistakes and winnings during the financial crisis of 2008.

Fast forward to today, I get to work and help many 50 to 70-year-olds plan for their retirement income. That is my biggest passion and what my company focuses on. It is also my mission to help people realize their financial dreams in retirement.

Retirement is such an interesting subject. There is so much that goes into planning one's retirement. The hardest and most interesting part is that not one person will have the same scenario as another person. Everyone is different. In order to retire, you need to know a lot of numbers. I'm going to break down the steps for you.

Your fixed expenses are number one! Most people would think they need a big account value in their investment balances. That definitely helps, but knowing your monthly fixed expenses is where it begins. You need to know if you have $3,000 or $5,000 a month of expenses. This includes your insurance bills, medications, property taxes, food, utilities and more. I think you get the idea of fixed expenses.

If you have $3,000 a month of fixed expenses, that means you have annual expenses of $36,000. Your social security may cover those expenses! That would be pretty amazing. If your month expenses are $5,000 going into retirement, that means that you will have $60,000 a year in fixed expenses. That's quite a bit more than $36,000!

When you know how much money you need every month, I am able to reverse engineer how to create income streams that could last your lifetime in retirement. It is pretty amazing.

In the $5,000 monthly expense example above, you may have $36,000 of social security payments per year. You now have an income gap of $24,000 a year! That is not a small sum of money.

This is where I come into play. When I work with my clients, we look to see how much money they have saved and invested during their working years. If they have saved $1,000,000, we created income from that million dollars to help close their income gap.

The reason for this is because it takes some of the emotions out of retirement planning. It actually helps calm people. When my clients agree to close their income gap, it gives them confidence. The confidence to Retire As You Desire.

That is so important.

There is an emotional and a physical toll that poor planning can take on your health. IF you have not saved enough money or have made poor investment decisions, you could really be in a bad emotional place. Money is very emotional.

Not having the money to pay your bills is such a drain on your mind, body and soul. It could lead to sickness as well. It is sad when this happens to people. But the reality is that it does happen, and quite often.

This is why I believe it is so important to figure out where your money is going now. Don't wait. Action is imperative. Your future, your health and your dreams could depend on it!

Speaking of dreams . . .

Dreaming is so much fun. People dream of retirement and their futures. What would you say your biggest dreams are? What would you like to do with your free time if you did not have to work and have money coming in to live off of?

You see, this is what retirement is about. But again, you don't have to wait until 65 to make this happen. It all comes down to your habits. our daily money habits.

I bet you're getting the theme of this book. **Consistency and action could lead to progress.** Progress turns into happiness. When you make progress toward your goals, you become happy. Happier than not acting on your goals and dreams.

I love dreaming and thinking of major things to accomplish. It is inspiring. We have one life to live, so why not dream big? This could mean an early retirement for some. Probably many. It could also mean having a million dollars saved. Or not having a mortgage. Or traveling to 10 new countries. The list is endless. As it should be.

Since we are living longer, we have more time to reach these goals. But to be able to do these things, your financial future depends on your habits.

I'd like you to take a moment to truly think about your life goals. Take some time to write them out. Write them down in this book. There is a spot here for you to do so. Start by listing 3 to 5 goals:

HERE ARE 3 TO 5 OF MY
GOALS & DREAMS

1.

2.

3.

4.

5.

Go ahead, do this now. Get your brain working. What would you like to accomplish in your lifetime?

I bet you have some big dreams. As do I!

When you go back to your list of goals and dreams, how many of them require money to get accomplished? **How much money would it take to accomplish all of these goals in your lifetime?**

Once you start to add up the costs, it could be an eye-opening experience for you. But in my mind, it's a good experience. **Your brain now will open up and begin thinking about how you could make these goals and dreams actually happen! That is the beauty of our brains.**

Pretend you would like to have a retirement home in Florida. Right on the water.

That sounds pretty amazing to me. I'd ask you; how could you afford this? How do you plan on paying for this?

Well, if you're 35, and if you put together a savings and investment plan, do you think you will have an opportunity to reach this goal?

My thoughts would be yes. It is feasible.

But if you're 60, and have not even started planning for retirement, it is going to be really difficult to make that dream a reality. A lot harder. As you have less and less time to set aside funds for their goal and less and less time for it to grow.

When I work with my soon to be retired clients, we always look at what their monthly expenses are.

We use a simple worksheet that makes it easy for them to figure out their true monthly expenses. If you would like a copy of this worksheet, send me an email at <u>bill@bloomfinancial.us</u> and my team will be happy to send it to you.

Knowing where you want to go will get your brain working. Your brain will think about how you can make your dreams happen.

Starting now could be your best opportunity for a bright financial future!

RETIRE AS YOU DESIRE MONEY TIPS

1. Time is our most important commodity.

2. Planning sooner rather than later makes it easier to achieve your goals.

3. Build money habits that support you.

4. What are your goals/dreams?

5. How much money is needed?

6. Build a plan toward the life you desire.

7. Build habits of putting funds toward your dreams.

READ THESE BOOKS, TOO!

Reading books has helped me immensely. It has literally changed my life. There have been so many books that I have read that has helped me change the way that I think. My habits have changed because of self-education and my life has as well. Luckily, some of these authors on my list I know personally. It is really an honor to be associated with some of these greats. Others, I would love to meet some day. For instance, Dan Sullivan created Strategic Coach. I've been in their business coaching programs for over seven years now. We get new books from them every quarter. I listed my favorite one below. I could create a list of books just from Dan Sullivan.

By reading my book, you have made it clear to yourself that you want to have a better financial life. A better future. By having a better financial life, you could alleviate some of the stress in your life that is tied to money. Again, money is a byproduct of how you want to live your life. You can take control of your financial future by implementing my tips and strategies.

I'm going to list some of my favorite books here and I would highly recommend that you pick up a copy of each of these:

Personality Isn't Permanent by Benjamin Hardy, PhD

Bluefishing by Steve Sims

Wanting What You Want by Dan Sullivan

Lifespan by David Sinclair, PhD

Epic Business by Justin Breen

Raving Fans by Ken Blanchard and Sheldon Bowles

Atomic Habits by James Clear

Stone Soup by Marcia Brown

The Go Giver by Bob Burg

Oh, The Places You'll Go by Dr. Seuss

I've written two other books: *Retire As You Desire* and The *Yachter's Guide to Early Retirement*. Also, don't forget to buy your copy of the Money Journal. This I believe is a critical step in your financial journey. The Money Journal was created to be paired with this book to give you the tools to succeed. If you want to continue learning about retirement planning and bettering your financial life, purchase your copy of my other three books on Amazon, and don't forget to get copies for your friends, family and co-workers that you know would benefit from reading these books.

Writing about finance is an absolute passion of mine. **Education should never stop. Don't stop learning. Self-education is such an important thing for your brain. Keep making progress. Every Single Day. Reading new books will help with learning who you are and what you really want out of life.**

If you would like more book suggestions, send me an email at <u>Bill@BloomFinancial.us</u> and I will send you some more titles of my other favorite books. I could list another 40 to 50 books, but these ten are a great starting point.

ABOUT THE AUTHOR

I am a husband and father. I am a writer in progress ☺. I'm an Amazon best-selling author. I've published three books and I'm currently working on the *Money Journal* to be released in 2020.

Retirement income is my favorite topic to talk about. I am a Retirement Income Certified Professional, RICP®. I love reading books, playing and watching soccer, sailing, sailboat racing, traveling with my family, and most importantly, spending time with my wife and son.

The reason that I am in business is for my clients. Retire As You Desire™ is my motto. My clients receive personalized retirement income plans. I help individuals, couples and business owners create lifetime income streams from their investments. I can show you techniques that may help you Retire As You Desire™ and live the lifestyle that you have always dreamed of in retirement.

Contact Info:

Bloom Financial

65 W. Jackson Blvd, Suite 109

Chicago, IL 60604

Office: (773) 326-8472

Email: Bill@BloomFinancial.us

www.BloomFinancialCo.com

www.RetireAsYouDesireScorecard.com

www.RetireAsYouDesireWorkshops.com